MAD LIBS®

#1 ORIGINAL MAD LIBS

By Roger Price and Leonard Stern

Mad Libs
An Imprint of Penguin Random House

MAD LIBS
Penguin Young Readers Group
An Imprint of Penguin Random House LLC

Concept created by Roger Price & Leonard Stern

Published by Mad Libs,
an imprint of Penguin Random House LLC,
345 Hudson Street, New York, New York 10014.
Printed in the USA.

ISBN 9780843100556
63 65 64

MAD LIBS®

INSTRUCTIONS

MAD LIBS® is a game for people who don't like games! It can be played by one, two, three, four, or forty.

• RIDICULOUSLY SIMPLE DIRECTIONS

In this tablet you will find stories containing blank spaces where words are left out. One player, the READER, selects one of these stories. The READER does not tell anyone what the story is about. Instead, he/she asks the other players, the WRITERS, to give him/her words. These words are used to fill in the blank spaces in the story.

• TO PLAY

The READER asks each WRITER in turn to call out a word—an adjective or a noun or whatever the space calls for—and uses them to fill in the blank spaces in the story. The result is a MAD LIBS® game.

When the READER then reads the completed MAD LIBS® game to the other players, they will discover that they have written a story that is fantastic, screamingly funny, shocking, silly, crazy, or just plain dumb—depending upon which words each WRITER called out.

• EXAMPLE (*Before* and *After*)

"________________ !" he said ________________
EXCLAMATION ADVERB

as he jumped into his convertible ________________ and
NOUN

drove off with his ________________ wife.
ADJECTIVE

"Ouch! !" he said stupidly
EXCLAMATION ADVERB

as he jumped into his convertible cat and
NOUN

drove off with his brave wife.
ADJECTIVE

MAD LIBS®
QUICK REVIEW

In case you have forgotten what adjectives, adverbs, nouns, and verbs are, here is a quick review:

An ADJECTIVE describes something or somebody. *Lumpy, soft, ugly, messy,* and *short* are adjectives.

An ADVERB tells how something is done. It modifies a verb and usually ends in "ly." *Modestly, stupidly, greedily,* and *carefully* are adverbs.

A NOUN is the name of a person, place or thing. *Sidewalk, umbrella, bridle, bathtub,* and *nose* are nouns.

A VERB is an action word. *Run, pitch, jump,* and *swim* are verbs. Put the verbs in past tense if the directions say PAST TENSE. *Ran, pitched, jumped,* and *swam* are verbs in the past tense.

When we ask for a PLACE, we mean any sort of place: a country or city *(Spain, Cleveland)* or a room *(bathroom, kitchen.)*

An EXCLAMATION or SILLY WORD is any sort of funny sound, gasp, grunt, or outcry, like *Wow!, Ouch!, Whomp!, Ick!,* and *Gadzooks!*

When we ask for specific words, like a NUMBER, a COLOR, an ANIMAL, or a PART OF THE BODY, we mean a word that is one of those things, like *seven, blue, horse,* or *head*.

When we ask for a PLURAL, it means more than one. For example, *cat* pluralized is *cats*.

MAD LIBS® is fun to play with friends, but you can also play it by yourself! To begin with, DO NOT look at the story on the page below. Fill in the blanks on this page with the words called for. Then, using the words you have selected, fill in the blank spaces in the story.

Now you've created your own hilarious MAD LIBS® game!

THE SPACE SHUTTLE

NOUN ____________

PLURAL NOUN ____________

VERB ENDING IN "ING" ____________

PLURAL NOUN ____________

CITY ____________

PLURAL NOUN ____________

ADJECTIVE ____________

NOUN ____________

NUMBER ____________

NOUN ____________

ADJECTIVE ____________

VERB ____________

VERB ____________

PLURAL NOUN ____________

VERB ENDING IN "ING" ____________

NUMBER ____________

ADVERB ____________

NOUN ____________

ADJECTIVE ____________

MAD LIBS®

THE SPACE SHUTTLE

In 1981, the U.S. launched the first real Space ______________ (NOUN). It was named *Columbia* and was piloted by two brave ______________ (PLURAL NOUN). They had practiced ______________ (VERB ENDING IN "ING") for two years and were expert ______________ (PLURAL NOUN). *Columbia* took off from ______________ (CITY) using its powerful first-stage ______________ (PLURAL NOUN) and soared off into the ______________ (ADJECTIVE) blue ______________ (NOUN). At an altitude of ______________ (NUMBER) feet, it went into orbit around the ______________ (NOUN). For people watching from Earth, it was a/an ______________ (ADJECTIVE) sight to ______________ (VERB)! Who could really ______________ (VERB) that there were two ______________ (PLURAL NOUN) in space? It was mind ______________ (VERB ENDING IN "ING"). After ______________ (NUMBER) orbits, the shuttle landed ______________ (ADVERB) at an air force ______________ (NOUN). It was a/an ______________ (ADJECTIVE) day for the U.S. Space Program.

MAD LIBS® is fun to play with friends, but you can also play it by yourself! To begin with, DO NOT look at the story on the page below. Fill in the blanks on this page with the words called for. Then, using the words you have selected, fill in the blank spaces in the story.

Now you've created your own hilarious MAD LIBS® game!

NEWSPAPER ARTICLE

ADJECTIVE ______________________________

ADJECTIVE ______________________________

ADJECTIVE ______________________________

NOUN ______________________________

NOUN ______________________________

VERB (PAST TENSE) ______________________________

COLOR ______________________________

EXCLAMATION ______________________________

ANIMAL ______________________________

MAD LIBS®

NEWSPAPER ARTICLE

Mrs. Fifi Vanderbold, the ____________ (ADJECTIVE) and ____________ (ADJECTIVE) heiress, has filed for divorce from her husband, Percy Vanderbold, the former ____________ (ADJECTIVE) ____________ (NOUN) of Harvard, class of '38, now in the ____________ (NOUN) business. Mrs. Vanderbold claimed that her husband had ____________ (VERB (PAST TENSE)) her bed of ____________ (COLOR) flowers and tracked ____________ (ADJECTIVE) mud into the house. He also criticized her cooking. Mr. Vanderbold, when asked to comment, said, "____________ (EXCLAMATION)! I didn't do it. The pet ____________ (ANIMAL) ruined the flowers. And I offered to take her out to restaurants more often!"

MAD LIBS® is fun to play with friends, but you can also play it by yourself! To begin with, DO NOT look at the story on the page below. Fill in the blanks on this page with the words called for. Then, using the words you have selected, fill in the blank spaces in the story.

Now you've created your own hilarious MAD LIBS® game!

DESCRIPTION OF THE LOVELY GROUP THAT I AM IN

ADJECTIVE ______________________

ADJECTIVE ______________________

PERSON IN ROOM ______________________

ADVERB ______________________

PLURAL NOUN ______________________

NUMBER ______________________

ADJECTIVE ______________________

ADVERB ______________________

ANOTHER PERSON IN ROOM ______________________

ADJECTIVE ______________________

NOUN ______________________

ANOTHER PERSON IN ROOM ______________________

NOUN ______________________

ADJECTIVE ______________________

ADJECTIVE ______________________

ADJECTIVE ______________________

ADJECTIVE ______________________

MAD LIBS®

DESCRIPTION OF THE LOVELY GROUP THAT I AM IN

We are having a perfectly ______________ (ADJECTIVE) time this evening in the ______________ (ADJECTIVE) home of ______________ (PERSON IN ROOM). The rooms are decorated ______________ (ADVERB) with many stylish ______________ (PLURAL NOUN) that must have cost at least ______________ (NUMBER) dollars. The guests are all ______________ (ADJECTIVE) conversationalists and are all ______________ (ADVERB) dressed. ______________ (ANOTHER PERSON IN ROOM) has been entertaining us by telling us about the time he/she showed his/her ______________ (ADJECTIVE) ______________ (NOUN) to ______________ (ANOTHER PERSON IN ROOM), who mistook it for an early American ______________ (NOUN). The refreshments are ______________ (ADJECTIVE), and the idea of serving hot and ______________ (ADJECTIVE) hors d'oeuvres showed imagination. Visiting here is always a/an ______________ (ADJECTIVE) experience!

MAD LIBS® is fun to play with friends, but you can also play it by yourself! To begin with, DO NOT look at the story on the page below. Fill in the blanks on this page with the words called for. Then, using the words you have selected, fill in the blank spaces in the story.

Now you've created your own hilarious MAD LIBS® game!

QUICK QUIZ

ADJECTIVE ____________________

NUMBER ____________________

GEOGRAPHICAL LOCATION ____________________

EXCLAMATION ____________________

NUMBER ____________________

ADJECTIVE ____________________

ADJECTIVE ____________________

PLURAL NOUN ____________________

ADVERB ____________________

ADJECTIVE ____________________

PERSON IN ROOM ____________________

NOUN ____________________

PLURAL NOUN ____________________

ADJECTIVE ____________________

NOUN ____________________

ANOTHER PERSON IN ROOM ____________________

MAD LIBS®
QUICK QUIZ

Who am I? I am a/an ____________ (ADJECTIVE) American. I was born ____________ (NUMBER) years ago in ____________ (GEOGRAPHICAL LOCATION). When my father first saw me, he said, "____________ (EXCLAMATION)!" I am ____________ (NUMBER) feet tall, have ____________ (ADJECTIVE) brown eyes, and a/an ____________ (ADJECTIVE) complexion. My hobby is collecting ____________ (PLURAL NOUN). I always speak ____________ (ADVERB), and I have made several ____________ (ADJECTIVE) motion pictures. I am married to ____________ (PERSON IN ROOM), the well-known Hollywood ____________ (NOUN). I have given away thousands of ____________ (PLURAL NOUN) to charity. My most prominent physical characteristics are my ____________ (ADJECTIVE) nose and my large ____________ (NOUN). Who am I?

ANSWER: I am ____________ (ANOTHER PERSON IN ROOM).

MAD LIBS® is fun to play with friends, but you can also play it by yourself! To begin with, DO NOT look at the story on the page below. Fill in the blanks on this page with the words called for. Then, using the words you have selected, fill in the blank spaces in the story.

Now you've created your own hilarious MAD LIBS® game!

ADVICE TO PROSPECTIVE PARENTS

ADJECTIVE ______________________

ADJECTIVE ______________________

NOUN ______________________

NOUN ______________________

NOUN ______________________

ADJECTIVE ______________________

NOUN ______________________

ADJECTIVE ______________________

PLURAL NOUN ______________________

NUMBER ______________________

PLURAL NOUN ______________________

ADVERB ______________________

NOUN ______________________

EXCLAMATION ______________________

NOUN ______________________

MAD LIBS®

ADVICE TO PROSPECTIVE PARENTS

Congratulations to all of you ____________ (ADJECTIVE) mothers and ____________ (ADJECTIVE) fathers. You are about to give birth to a/an ____________ (NOUN). Remember, a happy child comes from a happy ____________ (NOUN). The arrival of your ____________ (NOUN) will cause many ____________ (ADJECTIVE) changes in your life. You'll probably have to get up at four a.m. to give the little ____________ (NOUN) its bottle of ____________ (ADJECTIVE) milk and change his or her ____________ (PLURAL NOUN). Later, when he or she is ____________ (NUMBER) years old and able to walk, you'll hear the patter of little ____________ (PLURAL NOUN) around the house. And in no time, your child will be talking ____________ (ADVERB), and calling you his or her "____________ (NOUN)," and saying things like, "____________ (EXCLAMATION)!" right to your face. It's no wonder they are called little bundles of ____________ (NOUN).

MAD LIBS® is fun to play with friends, but you can also play it by yourself! To begin with, DO NOT look at the story on the page below. Fill in the blanks on this page with the words called for. Then, using the words you have selected, fill in the blank spaces in the story.

Now you've created your own hilarious MAD LIBS® game!

HOW TO SERVE WINE

ADVERB ____________________

ADJECTIVE ____________________

ADJECTIVE ____________________

PLURAL NOUN ____________________

NOUN ____________________

ADJECTIVE ____________________

ADJECTIVE ____________________

GEOGRAPHICAL LOCATION ____________________

PLURAL NOUN ____________________

ADJECTIVE ____________________

ADJECTIVE ____________________

ADJECTIVE ____________________

NOUN ____________________

PLURAL NOUN ____________________

ADVERB ____________________

ADJECTIVE ____________________

MAD LIBS®

HOW TO SERVE WINE

A good wine, served ________ (ADVERB), can make any meal a truly ________ (ADJECTIVE) occasion. The red wines have a/an ________ (ADJECTIVE) flavor that blends with boiled ________ (PLURAL NOUN) or smoked ________ (NOUN). White wines range in flavor from ________ (ADJECTIVE) to ________ (ADJECTIVE). The best wines are made by peasants in ________ (GEOGRAPHICAL LOCATION) from the juice of ripe ________ (PLURAL NOUN), by putting them in vats and squashing them with their ________ (ADJECTIVE) feet. This is what gives wine that ________ (ADJECTIVE) aroma. Here are a few rules:

1. Always serve white wine in a/an ________ (ADJECTIVE) glass at ________ (NOUN) temperature.
2. Never serve burgundy with fried ________ (PLURAL NOUN).
3. Wines should always be drunk ________ (ADVERB) or you're liable to end up with a/an ________ (ADJECTIVE) stomach.

MAD LIBS® is fun to play with friends, but you can also play it by yourself! To begin with, DO NOT look at the story on the page below. Fill in the blanks on this page with the words called for. Then, using the words you have selected, fill in the blank spaces in the story.

Now you've created your own hilarious MAD LIBS® game!

BOOK REVIEW

PERSON IN ROOM ______________________

NOUN ______________________

ADJECTIVE ______________________

NOUN ______________________

ADJECTIVE ______________________

ADJECTIVE ______________________

PERSON IN ROOM (FEMALE) ______________________

ADJECTIVE ______________________

NONSENSE WORD ______________________

NOUN ______________________

ADJECTIVE ______________________

NOUN ______________________

VERB ENDING IN "ING" ______________________

SAME PERSON (FEMALE) ______________________

ADJECTIVE ______________________

ADVERB ______________________

PRESTIGIOUS AWARD ______________________

MAD LIBS®
BOOK REVIEW

________________ (PERSON IN ROOM) has just written a book called "The ________ (NOUN) in the ________ (ADJECTIVE) ________ (NOUN)." The main character in this ________ (ADJECTIVE) story is a/an ________ (ADJECTIVE) woman named ________________ (PERSON IN ROOM (FEMALE)) who has just been elected president. She must decide whether to spend money on making ________ (ADJECTIVE) bombs, sending people to the planet ________ (NONSENSE WORD), or building ________ (NOUN) to accommodate the growing population. The author creates many ________ (ADJECTIVE) moments, and you will find yourself sitting on the edge of your ________ (NOUN) late at night because you cannot stop ________ (VERB ENDING IN "ING") this book. ________________ (SAME PERSON (FEMALE)) turns out to be the greatest president in the last century and leads the people to peace and ________ (ADJECTIVE). This book is written ________ (ADVERB) and should be nominated for a ________________ (PRESTIGIOUS AWARD).

MAD LIBS® is fun to play with friends, but you can also play it by yourself! To begin with, DO NOT look at the story on the page below. Fill in the blanks on this page with the words called for. Then, using the words you have selected, fill in the blank spaces in the story.

Now you've created your own hilarious MAD LIBS® game!

A STORY WITH A MORAL

PLURAL NOUN ______________________

PLURAL NOUN ______________________

ANIMAL (PLURAL) ______________________

ADJECTIVE ______________________

PLURAL NOUN ______________________

NOUN ______________________

VERB (PAST TENSE) ______________________

NOUN ______________________

SILLY WORD ______________________

PLURAL NOUN ______________________

SILLY WORD ______________________

SAME ANIMAL (PLURAL) ______________________

MAD LIBS®

A STORY WITH A MORAL

There once was a very cruel dictator. He would go into foreign ____________ (PLURAL NOUN) and bring back ______________ (PLURAL NOUN). He taxed his own people and made them give him ________________ (ANIMAL (PLURAL)) as payment for farming the land. Finally, some ___________ (ADJECTIVE) young ____________ (PLURAL NOUN) got fed up and organized a protest. They fought the oppression by carrying signs that said the dictator was a ___________ (NOUN). After many years of revolt, they finally _____________ (VERB (PAST TENSE)) the dictator. For punishment, he had to marry a __________ (NOUN) and live in _______________ (SILLY WORD) and sew little frilly __________ (PLURAL NOUN) for the rest of his life. The moral of this story is: A stitch in ______________ (SILLY WORD) saves ________________ (SAME ANIMAL (PLURAL)).

MAD LIBS® is fun to play with friends, but you can also play it by yourself! To begin with, DO NOT look at the story on the page below. Fill in the blanks on this page with the words called for. Then, using the words you have selected, fill in the blank spaces in the story.

Now you've created your own hilarious MAD LIBS® game!

BEAUTY ADVICE

ADJECTIVE ____________________

ADJECTIVE ____________________

PART OF THE BODY ____________________

NOUN ____________________

TYPE OF CONTAINER ____________________

TYPE OF LIQUID ____________________

NOUN ____________________

NOUN ____________________

ADJECTIVE ____________________

ADJECTIVE ____________________

NOUN ____________________

ADJECTIVE ____________________

ADJECTIVE ____________________

ADJECTIVE ____________________

ADVERB ____________________

ADJECTIVE ____________________

PERSON IN ROOM ____________________

MAD LIBS®

BEAUTY ADVICE

If your skin is ________ (ADJECTIVE) or ________ (ADJECTIVE), you can cure this condition with the following regimen. Every morning, before washing your ________ (PART OF THE BODY), massage it gently with a/an ________ (NOUN) that has been soaked overnight in a/an ________ (TYPE OF CONTAINER) full of warm ________ (TYPE OF LIQUID). Then mix together some ________ (NOUN) and some ________ (NOUN) until the mixture becomes ________ (ADJECTIVE), and pat this onto your ________ (ADJECTIVE) face for five minutes. Then remove, using a/an ________ (NOUN), and wash your face with ________ (ADJECTIVE) water. Do not omit this ________ (ADJECTIVE) step, or your skin will become ________ (ADJECTIVE). Do this ________ (ADVERB) every day, and you will soon be as ________ (ADJECTIVE) as ________ (PERSON IN ROOM).

MAD LIBS® is fun to play with friends, but you can also play it by yourself! To begin with, DO NOT look at the story on the page below. Fill in the blanks on this page with the words called for. Then, using the words you have selected, fill in the blank spaces in the story.

Now you've created your own hilarious MAD LIBS® game!

NEWSPAPER ADS

ADJECTIVE ________________

ADJECTIVE ________________

ADJECTIVE ________________

ADVERB ________________

ADJECTIVE ________________

NOUN ________________

NOUN ________________

ADJECTIVE ________________

ADJECTIVE ________________

ADJECTIVE ________________

NOUN ________________

NOUN ________________

GEOGRAPHICAL LOCATION ________________

ADJECTIVE ________________

ADJECTIVE ________________

ADJECTIVE ________________

PERSON IN ROOM ________________

NOUN ________________

ADJECTIVE ________________

MAD LIBS®

NEWSPAPER ADS

FOR SALE: 1957 Sedan. This ____________ (ADJECTIVE) car is in a/an ____________ (ADJECTIVE) condition. It was formerly owned by a/an ____________ (ADJECTIVE) schoolteacher who always drove it ____________ (ADVERB). There is a/an ____________ (ADJECTIVE) ____________ (NOUN) in the back seat and a chrome ____________ (NOUN) on the hood. It has a/an ____________ (ADJECTIVE) paint job, ____________ (ADJECTIVE) tires, and the back opens out into a/an ____________ (ADJECTIVE) ____________ (NOUN). Will consider taking slightly used ____________ (NOUN) in trade.

LOST: In the vicinity of ____________ (GEOGRAPHICAL LOCATION), a/an ____________ (ADJECTIVE) French poodle with ____________ (ADJECTIVE) hair and a/an ____________ (ADJECTIVE) tail. It answers to the name of ____________ (PERSON IN ROOM) and when last seen was carrying a/an ____________ (NOUN) in its mouth. A/An ____________ (ADJECTIVE) reward is offered.

MAD LIBS® is fun to play with friends, but you can also play it by yourself! To begin with, DO NOT look at the story on the page below. Fill in the blanks on this page with the words called for. Then, using the words you have selected, fill in the blank spaces in the story.

Now you've created your own hilarious MAD LIBS® game!

FABLE #1

ADJECTIVE ______________________

NOUN ______________________

PERSON IN ROOM ______________________

ADJECTIVE ______________________

ADJECTIVE ______________________

ADJECTIVE ______________________

EXCLAMATION ______________________

ADVERB ______________________

NOUN ______________________

ADJECTIVE ______________________

NOUN ______________________

ADVERB ______________________

ADJECTIVE ______________________

ADJECTIVE ______________________

NOUN ______________________

NOUN ______________________

EXCLAMATION ______________________

ADJECTIVE ______________________

NOUN ______________________

NOUN ______________________

NOUN ______________________

NOUN ______________________

NOUN ______________________

MAD LIBS®

FABLE #1

Once upon a time, a/an ____________ (ADJECTIVE) ____________ (NOUN) expert named ____________ (PERSON IN ROOM) felt a/an ____________ (ADJECTIVE) pain. He sent for a/an ____________ (ADJECTIVE) surgeon who looked at his ____________ (ADJECTIVE) stomach and said, "____________ (EXCLAMATION)!" Then he muttered ____________ (ADVERB), "I see your trouble. The ____________ (NOUN) on your ____________ (ADJECTIVE) stomach is overlapping the ____________ (NOUN) next to your kidney." The surgeon ____________ (ADVERB) took him to the ____________ (ADJECTIVE) operating room of the hospital. There he made a/an ____________ (ADJECTIVE) incision reaching from the patient's ____________ (NOUN) to his ____________ (NOUN). "____________ (EXCLAMATION)!" said the surgeon. "That takes care of that ____________ (ADJECTIVE) ____________ (NOUN)." With that, he began sewing up the incision. However, on the tenth stitch the patient sneezed and almost pulled the ____________ (NOUN) out of the ____________ (NOUN), but the surgeon took one final stitch and saved the ____________ (NOUN). MORAL: A/An ____________ (NOUN) in time saves nine.

MAD LIBS® is fun to play with friends, but you can also play it by yourself! To begin with, DO NOT look at the story on the page below. Fill in the blanks on this page with the words called for. Then, using the words you have selected, fill in the blank spaces in the story.

Now you've created your own hilarious MAD LIBS® game!

MY DREAM MAN

ADJECTIVE ____________________

ADJECTIVE ____________________

CELEBRITY ____________________

ANOTHER CELEBRITY ____________________

ANIMAL ____________________

VERB ____________________

NOUN ____________________

NOUN ____________________

PART OF THE BODY ____________________

ADVERB ____________________

ADJECTIVE ____________________

ADVERB ____________________

ADJECTIVE ____________________

ADJECTIVE ____________________

PART OF THE BODY ____________________

ADJECTIVE ____________________

NOUN ____________________

ADJECTIVE ____________________

PERSON IN ROOM (MALE) ____________________

MAD LIBS®

MY DREAM MAN

My "Dream Man" should, first of all, be very ____________ (ADJECTIVE) and ____________ (ADJECTIVE). He should have a physique like ____________ (CELEBRITY), a profile like ____________ (ANOTHER CELEBRITY), and the intelligence of a/an ____________ (ANIMAL). He must be polite and always remember to ____________ (VERB) my ____________ (NOUN), to tip his ____________ (NOUN), and to take my ____________ (PART OF THE BODY) when crossing the street. He should move ____________ (ADVERB), should have a/an ____________ (ADJECTIVE) voice, and should always dress ____________ (ADVERB). I would also like him to be a/an ____________ (ADJECTIVE) dancer, and when we're alone, he should whisper ____________ (ADJECTIVE) nothings in my ____________ (PART OF THE BODY) and hold my ____________ (ADJECTIVE) ____________ (NOUN). I know a/an ____________ (ADJECTIVE) man like this is hard to find. In fact, the only one I can think of is ____________ (PERSON IN ROOM (MALE)).

MAD LIBS® is fun to play with friends, but you can also play it by yourself! To begin with, DO NOT look at the story on the page below. Fill in the blanks on this page with the words called for. Then, using the words you have selected, fill in the blank spaces in the story.

Now you've created your own hilarious MAD LIBS® game!

HOW TO GO TO SLEEP

ADJECTIVE ____________________

ADJECTIVE ____________________

TYPE OF LIQUID ____________________

ADJECTIVE ____________________

ADJECTIVE ____________________

ADVERB ____________________

ADJECTIVE ____________________

PLURAL NOUN ____________________

ADJECTIVE ____________________

ADJECTIVE ____________________

PLURAL NOUN ____________________

NOUN ____________________

PLURAL NOUN ____________________

NOUN ____________________

ADJECTIVE ____________________

ADJECTIVE ____________________

PART OF THE BODY ____________________

MAD LIBS®

HOW TO GO TO SLEEP

If you have trouble falling asleep, you probably have a/an ____________ (ADJECTIVE) mind. You must learn to relax so you will have a/an ____________ (ADJECTIVE) mind instead. First, drink a cup of hot ____________ (TYPE OF LIQUID) and stretch out on a/an ____________ (ADJECTIVE) bed in a/an ____________ (ADJECTIVE) position. Then, breathe ____________ (ADVERB) and think about something beautiful, such as ____________ (ADJECTIVE) ____________ (PLURAL NOUN). Do not think about your ____________ (ADJECTIVE) enemies or entertain any other ____________ (ADJECTIVE) thoughts. Concentrate on something restful, such as ____________ (PLURAL NOUN), which will make your ____________ (NOUN) more relaxed, or count imaginary ____________ (PLURAL NOUN) jumping over a/an ____________ (NOUN). Follow these ____________ (ADJECTIVE) rules and you will fall into a/an ____________ (ADJECTIVE) sleep the minute your ____________ (PART OF THE BODY) hits the pillow.

MAD LIBS® is fun to play with friends, but you can also play it by yourself! To begin with, DO NOT look at the story on the page below. Fill in the blanks on this page with the words called for. Then, using the words you have selected, fill in the blank spaces in the story.

Now you've created your own hilarious MAD LIBS® game!

FABLE #2

PLURAL NOUN ____________

ADJECTIVE ____________

PERSON IN ROOM (MALE) ____________

ADJECTIVE ____________

NOUN ____________

NOUN ____________

ADJECTIVE ____________

NOUN ____________

NOUN ____________

ADJECTIVE ____________

ADJECTIVE ____________

ADVERB ____________

NOUN ____________

PLURAL NOUN ____________

NOUN ____________

ADJECTIVE ____________

NOUN ____________

NOUN ____________

MAD LIBS®

FABLE #2

Once upon a time, there was a very curious girl who was always poking her nose into everybody's ____________ (PLURAL NOUN). She kept company with a/an ____________ (ADJECTIVE) man named ____________ (PERSON IN ROOM (MALE)), who was always buying her ____________ (ADJECTIVE) presents. Once he gave her a diamond ____________ (NOUN) to wear on her ____________ (NOUN), and he bought her a/an ____________ (ADJECTIVE) ____________ (NOUN) to wear in her ____________ (NOUN). Then one day he bought her a/an ____________ (ADJECTIVE) horse. As soon as she saw the ____________ (ADJECTIVE) animal, she began to examine it ____________ (ADVERB). First, she looked at the horse's ____________ (NOUN) and then at its ____________ (PLURAL NOUN). Then she opened its mouth so she could look at its ____________ (NOUN). At this, the horse became ____________ (ADJECTIVE) and bit off her ____________ (NOUN).

MORAL: Never look a gift horse in the ____________ (NOUN).

MAD LIBS® is fun to play with friends, but you can also play it by yourself! To begin with, DO NOT look at the story on the page below. Fill in the blanks on this page with the words called for. Then, using the words you have selected, fill in the blank spaces in the story.

Now you've created your own hilarious MAD LIBS® game!

ARMY INFORMATION

ADJECTIVE ____________________

ADJECTIVE ____________________

PLURAL NOUN ____________________

PLURAL NOUN ____________________

NOUN ____________________

NOUN ____________________

ADVERB ____________________

ADJECTIVE ____________________

PLURAL NOUN ____________________

NOUN ____________________

PLURAL NOUN ____________________

ADJECTIVE ____________________

EXCLAMATION ____________________

NOUN ____________________

NOUN ____________________

ADJECTIVE ____________________

NOUN ____________________

MAD LIBS®

ARMY INFORMATION

If you plan on joining the army, here are some ______________ (ADJECTIVE) hints that will help you become a/an ______________ (ADJECTIVE) soldier. The army is made up of officers, non-coms, and ______________ (PLURAL NOUN). You can recognize an officer by the ______________ (NOUN) on his shoulders and the ______________ (NOUN) on his cap. When you address an officer, always say, "______________ (NOUN)" and salute ______________ (ADVERB). If you get a/an ______________ (ADJECTIVE) haircut, keep your ______________ (PLURAL NOUN) shined, and see that your ______________ (NOUN) is clean at all times, you will be a credit to the slogan, "the Army builds ______________ (PLURAL NOUN)." And at roll call, when the ______________ (ADJECTIVE) sergeant calls your name, shout "______________ (EXCLAMATION)!" loud and clear. Also, become familiar with basic weapons such as the thirty-calibre ______________ (NOUN) and the automatic ______________ (NOUN). Follow this advice and in no time you'll win the ______________ (ADJECTIVE) Conduct ______________ (NOUN).

MAD LIBS® is fun to play with friends, but you can also play it by yourself! To begin with, DO NOT look at the story on the page below. Fill in the blanks on this page with the words called for. Then, using the words you have selected, fill in the blank spaces in the story.

Now you've created your own hilarious MAD LIBS® game!

TRAVEL SUGGESTION

ADJECTIVE ____________________

ADJECTIVE ____________________

ADJECTIVE ____________________

ADJECTIVE ____________________

PLURAL NOUN ____________________

PLURAL NOUN ____________________

ADJECTIVE ____________________

NOUN ____________________

PLURAL NOUN ____________________

NOUN ____________________

NOUN ____________________

ADJECTIVE ____________________

ADJECTIVE ____________________

ADJECTIVE ____________________

ADJECTIVE ____________________

ADJECTIVE ____________________

NOUN ____________________

ADJECTIVE ____________________

MAD LIBS®

TRAVEL SUGGESTION

If you're looking for a place to spend a/an ________________ (ADJECTIVE) honey-moon, think of ________________ (ADJECTIVE) Mexico. There, under a brilliant, ________________ (ADJECTIVE) sky, you and your ________________ (ADJECTIVE) bride can spend hours inspecting the quaint ________________ (PLURAL NOUN) and the ancient Aztec ________________ (PLURAL NOUN). You will be fascinated by the ________________ (ADJECTIVE) customs of the natives. In the evening, you can retire to the local ____________ (NOUN), which is what the Mexicans call their ____________ (PLURAL NOUN), and watch the famous ____________ (NOUN) dance called the ____________ (NOUN). Hotels there have all ________________ (ADJECTIVE) conveniences, including ________________ (ADJECTIVE) water, ________________ (ADJECTIVE) air-conditioning, and ____________ (ADJECTIVE) service. The rates are also very ____________ (ADJECTIVE). In a few days, you and your bride will be lolling on the ____________ (NOUN), just like the ________________ (ADJECTIVE) natives.

MAD LIBS® is fun to play with friends, but you can also play it by yourself! To begin with, DO NOT look at the story on the page below. Fill in the blanks on this page with the words called for. Then, using the words you have selected, fill in the blank spaces in the story.

Now you've created your own hilarious MAD LIBS® game!

DESCRIPTION OF WEDDING

ADJECTIVE ____________________

ADJECTIVE ____________________

PERSON IN ROOM (FEMALE) ____________________

PERSON IN ROOM (MALE) ____________________

ADVERB ____________________

ADJECTIVE ____________________

NOUN ____________________

ADJECTIVE ____________________

ADJECTIVE ____________________

ADJECTIVE ____________________

NOUN ____________________

ADJECTIVE ____________________

NOUN ____________________

ADJECTIVE ____________________

ADJECTIVE ____________________

ADJECTIVE ____________________

ADJECTIVE ____________________

PLURAL NOUN ____________________

GEOGRAPHICAL LOCATION ____________________

ADVERB ____________________

MAD LIBS®

DESCRIPTION OF WEDDING

The ________ (ADJECTIVE) wedding yesterday afternoon between ________ (ADJECTIVE) ________________ (PERSON IN ROOM (FEMALE)) and her groom, ________________ (PERSON IN ROOM (MALE)), was carried off ____________ (ADVERB). The bride wore a long ____________ (ADJECTIVE) __________ (NOUN) with ____________ (ADJECTIVE) edging and a/an ____________ (ADJECTIVE) neckline. At the end of the ____________ (ADJECTIVE) ceremony, there wasn't a dry ____________ (NOUN) in the place. Later, at the reception, the bride's mother said, "The groom is a/an ____________ (ADJECTIVE) man, just the type of ____________ (NOUN) we wanted for our ____________ (ADJECTIVE) daughter." The ____________ (ADJECTIVE) couple left midst a flurry of ____________ (ADJECTIVE) congratulations, to spend a/an ____________ (ADJECTIVE) honeymoon visiting ____________ (PLURAL NOUN) in ________________ (GEOGRAPHICAL LOCATION). They are sure to live ____________ (ADVERB) for many years.

MAD LIBS® is fun to play with friends, but you can also play it by yourself! To begin with, DO NOT look at the story on the page below. Fill in the blanks on this page with the words called for. Then, using the words you have selected, fill in the blank spaces in the story.

Now you've created your own hilarious MAD LIBS® game!

MY DREAM GIRL

ADJECTIVE ____________________

COLOR ____________________

PLURAL NOUN ____________________

ADJECTIVE ____________________

TYPE OF LIQUID ____________________

ADJECTIVE ____________________

PLURAL NOUN ____________________

ADJECTIVE ____________________

NOUN ____________________

PERSON IN ROOM ____________________

EXCLAMATION ____________________

ADJECTIVE ____________________

ADJECTIVE ____________________

ADJECTIVE ____________________

ADJECTIVE ____________________

NOUN ____________________

PLURAL NOUN ____________________

ADJECTIVE ____________________

PERSON IN ROOM (FEMALE) ____________________

MAD LIBS®

MY DREAM GIRL

The girl of my dreams has ________ (ADJECTIVE) ________ (COLOR) hair scented like ________ (PLURAL NOUN). Her eyes are like two ________ (ADJECTIVE) pools of ________ (TYPE OF LIQUID). And her lips remind me of ________ (ADJECTIVE) ________ (PLURAL NOUN). Her skin is as smooth and lovely as a/an ________ (ADJECTIVE) ________ (NOUN), and she has a figure like ________ (PERSON IN ROOM). When she enters a room, people always stare at her and say, "________ (EXCLAMATION)! What a/an ________ (ADJECTIVE) woman!" Her sense of humor is always ________ (ADJECTIVE), and people marvel at her ________ (ADJECTIVE) vocabulary. In my dreams I see her wearing a/an ________ (ADJECTIVE) dress and a diamond ________ (NOUN) in her hair. I would gladly give up all my ________ (PLURAL NOUN) for one evening with this ________ (ADJECTIVE) female. Her name is ________ (PERSON IN ROOM (FEMALE)).

MAD LIBS® is fun to play with friends, but you can also play it by yourself! To begin with, DO NOT look at the story on the page below. Fill in the blanks on this page with the words called for. Then, using the words you have selected, fill in the blank spaces in the story.

Now you've created your own hilarious MAD LIBS® game!

FABLE #3

ADJECTIVE ____________________

ADJECTIVE ____________________

ADJECTIVE ____________________

ADJECTIVE ____________________

EXCLAMATION ____________________

ADJECTIVE ____________________

ADJECTIVE ____________________

ADJECTIVE ____________________

ADJECTIVE ____________________

ADJECTIVE ____________________

ADVERB ____________________

NOUN ____________________

NOUN ____________________

NOUN ____________________

MAD LIBS®

FABLE #3

Once upon a time, a/an ______________ (ADJECTIVE) dog got hold of a/an ______________ (ADJECTIVE) bone. He was walking across a/an ______________ (ADJECTIVE) bridge and saw his ______________ (ADJECTIVE) reflection in the water. "______________ (EXCLAMATION)!" he said. "There is another ______________ (ADJECTIVE) dog with another ______________ (ADJECTIVE) bone. I'll make a/an ______________ (ADJECTIVE) grab, take his, and then I'll have two ______________ (ADJECTIVE) bones." With that the ______________ (ADJECTIVE) dog jumped into the water and ______________ (ADVERB) drowned. MORAL: A/An ______________ (NOUN) in the ______________ (NOUN) is worth two in the ______________ (NOUN).

MAD LIBS® is fun to play with friends, but you can also play it by yourself! To begin with, DO NOT look at the story on the page below. Fill in the blanks on this page with the words called for. Then, using the words you have selected, fill in the blank spaces in the story.

Now you've created your own hilarious MAD LIBS® game!

PROPER CARE OF THE SCALP

ADJECTIVE ____________________

ADJECTIVE ____________________

ADJECTIVE ____________________

ADJECTIVE ____________________

NOUN ____________________

PLURAL NOUN ____________________

ADVERB ____________________

ADJECTIVE ____________________

NOUN ____________________

NOUN ____________________

NOUN ____________________

ADJECTIVE ____________________

NOUN ____________________

NOUN ____________________

MAD LIBS®

PROPER CARE OF THE SCALP

Don't neglect your scalp! Even though you don't know it, your scalp may be ______________ (ADJECTIVE). This can cause your hair to turn ______________ (ADJECTIVE) and ______________ (ADJECTIVE). A/An ______________ (ADJECTIVE) scalp is due to overactivity on the part of the ______________ (NOUN) gland and to excessive production of the ______________ (PLURAL NOUN) normally present in the skin. For a healthy scalp, wash your head ______________ (ADVERB) every night in ______________ (ADJECTIVE) water and then take a hot ______________ (NOUN) shampoo. Then massage your ______________ (NOUN) for five minutes with a sharp ______________ (NOUN). If you suffer from ______________ (ADJECTIVE) hair, soak your ______________ (NOUN) regularly in a/an ______________ (NOUN) of vinegar. Good luck!

MAD LIBS® is fun to play with friends, but you can also play it by yourself! To begin with, DO NOT look at the story on the page below. Fill in the blanks on this page with the words called for. Then, using the words you have selected, fill in the blank spaces in the story.

Now you've created your own hilarious MAD LIBS® game!

A (SECRET) LETTER FROM AN ADMIRER

PERSON IN ROOM (FEMALE) ____________

NOUN ____________

ADJECTIVE ____________

ADJECTIVE ____________

ANOTHER PERSON IN ROOM ____________

ADJECTIVE ____________

ADJECTIVE ____________

PLURAL NOUN ____________

ADJECTIVE ____________

ADJECTIVE ____________

ADJECTIVE ____________

ADJECTIVE ____________

ADJECTIVE ____________

ADJECTIVE ____________

ADJECTIVE ____________

ADJECTIVE ____________

ADJECTIVE ____________

NOUN ____________

ADVERB ____________

PERSON IN ROOM (MALE) ____________

MAD LIBS®

A (SECRET) LETTER FROM AN ADMIRER

Dear Miss ______________ (PERSON IN ROOM (FEMALE)),

You may not recall my ______________ (NOUN), but I met you at the ______________ (ADJECTIVE) cocktail party given by our ______________ (ADJECTIVE) friend, ______________ (ANOTHER PERSON IN ROOM). We had a/an ______________ (ADJECTIVE) talk about ______________ (ADJECTIVE) ______________ (PLURAL NOUN), and I was impressed by your ______________ (ADJECTIVE) conversation and your grasp of the ______________ (ADJECTIVE) situation. Also, I was very much attracted by your ______________ (ADJECTIVE) eyes, your ______________ (ADJECTIVE) little chin, and your ______________ (ADJECTIVE) teeth. If you'll pardon me for seeming ______________ (ADJECTIVE), I was fascinated by your ______________ (ADJECTIVE) walk and by your ______________ (ADJECTIVE) figure. I hope I made a/an ______________ (ADJECTIVE) impression and that we can get together for a nice ______________ (NOUN) next week.

______________ (ADVERB) yours,

______________ (PERSON IN ROOM (MALE))